Weeds, Dreams, & Flowers

To Tom —
Long Time,
Long Road

All best to you —

Warmly!
Halin

8/2011

Weeds, Dreams, & Flowers

Halim Dunsky

Epigraph Books
Rhinebeck, New York

Back cover photo: Lisa Fladager

Printed in the United States of America

Epigraph Books
27 Lamoree Road
Rhinebeck, New York 12572
www.epigraphPS.com
USA 845-876-4861

ISBN 978-0-9830517-9-4

Library of Congress Control Number: 2011920017

The shadows frame the light.

—Phil Ochs

We work to find the One inside
that is unconditioned by any idea.

—Sufi Murshida Khadija

All our relations are asking for our deepest realization.

—Murshid Wali Ali Meyer

Aho! Mitakoye Oyasin.

Contents

Intimations

A thin black ribbon
 like a winding strip of asphalt
  suspended in darkness
   not bound to the known earth
    carries me forward
     under an arch of darkness
      from darkness into darkness

Huge forms of incomprehensible shape
 pass at the edges of visibility
  their contours only hinted
   by dimly glowing whispers of red
    (called up as though by coals)
     that flare, slide, and vanish

Bridge building and demolition
 are rumored in distant flashes of hot light.
  Alien engines and their keepers
   are wielding the piercing torches of reassembly
    in a spatter of sparks not heard,
     silent as an illumination of clouds
      storm-lit from beyond the horizon

My Patience

I.

little boy
learning to stand
suspended by the head

who will be surprised
when you wither

II.

sad goddess
always recalling
the sweet chocolate moon

only blood time
will unlock your mad beauty

III.

white swan
you are so proud
of your long neck

but my tears are longer

IV.

this heavy rock
which I call my patience
has many names

beneath it
a great longing
flutters

The Need to Weep

the need to weep is greater even
than our own huge stories make it

the tears we have not let
are seeping from the earth now
softening our footing everywhere

are you standing on a dry spot?
not for long

be careful where you step

soon you won't have anywhere to go

| 4 |

Poet

> "If you are a poet, you will see clearly that there is a
> cloud floating in this sheet of paper."
>
> —Thich Nhat Hanh

If you see a cloud
in this paper, signify
by saying, "poet."

We have seen a cloud
in this paper, in our eyes,
and we say, "poet."

Cloud, paper, eyes, heart—
say "poet" and disappear.
Plum blossom snow fall.

Mountains for Donovan

When conditions are right
            (stay with me now)
        a certain angle of light
        a certain level of dust and humidity
the color of the sky above the mountains
becomes wholly the same
as the blue of the mountain flanks
        below the sharp snowcaps

At these secret moments of conjunction
all we have is an avatar of white peaks

The mountains are gone

In the empty space
behind that floating

my heart breathes

Gladiolus

We danced in the ravine this morning
amid a choreography of trees
holding this little valley
safe in the fogs of winter

a scratch in the earth
perpetuating against the suburbs
a remnant of slow time

We write in the cafe this afternoon
Green stalks of gladiolus arch and angle,
dance in a rhythm we barely remember

Luminous red flowers
bright trumpet shouts of blood
move imperceptibly,
open, reach, shrivel and grow dark
at a pace so slow
only a lover can apprehend it

While we bathe in noise,
while we shiver and vibrate,
caging the panic with talk too loud,
living too fast for our short time,
these flowers, gone already
live longer than we do

Where the Mercy Is Kept

dear
    ann landers
i have this friend,
    see,
        who wants to know...

my friend had
    to kill
        his enemy

his life
    had flowed
until it hardened
    to the shape
        of that act alone
that act
    uniquely
        alone

in his hand
    the base
        of a broken lightbulb
laid open
    that blocked
        incontestable
        throat

his face
    was washed in blood

we really need…
  my friend…
    i need

a gentler way
  of opening

sweet
  ann landers
can your experts
  tell you
where the mercy
  is kept

How grim are your lips,
morning dog walker, striding
in your destiny

Poems can't get out
when mind is turning, thumping
like a clothes dryer!

Why Does the Day Resist Us?

In Seattle, winter mornings begin black,
lighten to pearl grey, then dove grey

and then stay that way
for the rest of the week

Fog water fills the hollows of the air
Fat raindrops like beetles strike my windshield

So many hunched shoulders hurry by
so many stiff necks push ahead
into the cold, resisting day

As long as we are turned away
from our true work
the day will spit us out

This is the same movement
as our turning away

Dry Leaves

My life blows past like dry leaves
and scraps of paper on a winter wind.
Unpaid bills and debts of conscience
swirl around my shoulders
and race ahead
down the narrowing tunnel of the future
where I will meet them
later

The wind is impatient—
it pushes at my back—
but in my heavy coat
I hunch against the cold.
Collar lifted,
fists buried deep in pockets,
elbows pulled close,
I begrudge each forward step

Shhhh…

I am listening for the
vibrations in my solid body.
I am hunting
the elusive frequency,
that one that will render me
transparent to the wind

To Live, With the Memory

From a hidden boneyard
rising out of ribs
an ectoplasmic essence hovers,
holds the recall of injustice,
will not rest.

And does this revenant travel
to visit with nightmares
the poacher's fitful sleep?

He waves flies from his eyes
and elephants from his dreams
with equal unsuccess.

Pay attention!
This poem is not about elephants.

Lot's Wife

We're making a video about Lot's wife,
who turned back for one last look
at what she'd been.
I've wondered at her state of mind—
was she unsure? bereft? defiant?

In any case, she's dead today,
skeletal and stark, all salt.
(I licked her to be sure.)

The crew is all women but me.
The director reminds me I'm not here
to make love to Lot's wife,
though Lot is long gone.

At lunch I tear white chicken flesh with my teeth.

Lot's wife makes me shiver
in the sharp lighting.
We're showing her with ropes,
hanged and fearsome
Man's justice
tagging after God's.

I come close again to touch her cheek.
She breathes

Deep Is Not Enough

A thin light comes through our window.

Captain Nemo and I,
we muse over brandy in our warm lounge,
surrounded by elegant appointments of brass
and rare woods, golden oil lamps,
brocades and crystal.

Outside, cold greens
undulate quietly
in a breeze that flows
through the fingers of the trees.

We descend through
fathoms of cold leaf-water.

Our window spills lemon,
draws the slow attention of the trees.

They grow taller, making us deeper,
they stare a while, they are cool,
their feeling is disdain.

Engines of misfortune carry us
into realms we endlessly penetrate
but never touch.

We are protected, we are insulated,
we are isolated, we are trapped.

Birds swim by.

Social Workers of the Inward City

The mother was concerned about the child,
      who liked to sleep in a bowl on the porch.
But the bowl was empty.
There was just a little bit of egg yolk in it.

We wanted to help the child.

The cat had a spot of blood on its chest.
Had it eaten the child?
We applied fluid to the spot, which dissolved a bit,
      but the child did not appear.

The mother said the child was dead in the bedroom,
But we knew the child was still alive,
      and though he would not show himself,
      he listened.

His need to speak had overpowered him,
      leaving only silence.
We showed him how to find his voice in a drumhead.

One Morning

One morning
instead of waiting for the bus
I dropped down on all fours and crawled
for many blocks

The ground was cool and moist
My eyes and nose were inches
from the pavement
I sniffed through yards and gardens
meeting every little rock and plant

When I got up, I was covered with green
from the grass and the moss

After this, a social service agency
placed me in a foster home
They took me away
from my wife and children

They said I was a mutant
who suffered from being sad,
and sentenced me
to play for four years

I found a huge wall of earth under a bridge
full of numbered doors to explore

What the Dream Said

I was nearly blind, but finally I ran away from home
    to seek my fortune.

I left my mother a defiant note, scrawled with
    letters outside and across the little boxes
    on the form.

And out I went, tapping firmly with my cane.

I crossed the yard to the chauffeur's cottage
    and made him get up to take me away.
His girlfriend was the most beautiful girl in the world.
(My eyes were getting better already.)

The chauffeur and the girl were fooling around.
I said I didn't pay him so I could wait around while he
    fooled around.
If I was going to be waiting, at least she would be
    fooling around
    with me.
And she let me kiss her and touch her breast a little.

We got into the car.
He brought my special cripple's bicycle and put it in the
    trunk, which was very thoughtful.
He was my brother, and the size of four people.

So we set out, but soon they were gone and I was walking.

A crowd was gathered by a tall building that people were
        trapped in.
Onlookers bedded down for the night in the plaza.
It was crowded, body to body. We stayed awake a long time.
The older man next to me was friendly, explaining things.

People were dropping treasures out of the building
        to save them, including baskets of food, clothes,
        and babies.
There was a lot of joking and calling out as things were
        caught and piled up,
            shared out, or cared for.

Some people were singing the King's original folk music.

In the tree above me, a fantastic fox-like animal
        with rich black and white fur
        ate a bird
        in the moonlight.

In the morning I woke early, and started packing up my
        things.
Everybody's stuff was piled together, but I managed to sort
        mine out.
Some of my towels and underwear were wet.
There were also some pairs of underwear caked with shit,
        but those weren't mine.
I was surprised to see how dirty some people let themselves
        get, and I wondered if they were sick.

I started on my way again, and I thought, this is almost perfect.
If only I had a knapsack instead of this carry bag.

And somebody came along and traded his knapsack for my
bag.
As I was putting my dress shirts into my new knapsack,
I noticed I had not brought along my collar stays.
My friends taught me how to materialize small objects.
At first I kept getting broken or mismatched ones, but
eventually I got the hang of it.

My friends taught me more magic, so that I was able to keep
dirt off my clothes and really take care of myself to
stay safe.

We came to a town, and started climbing on roofs.
I did a very difficult traverse
across some colorful ledges and facades.
I was scared, but I knew if I got in trouble,
I could use my magic to not fall.
But actually I used only my fingers and toes and smarts and
strength to do the climbing.

I caught up with my friends on one roof.
We watched some war veterans returning home and were
amazed to see that they were just regular people.

Some of the soldiers were hurt.
We friends made a pact to secretly help them, and always use
our powers for good.

We began to send them secret support.

Ash Man

Let's not talk about everybody else's goddam ideas
Let's not talk about how people this or society that
I want to hear about you
I want you to talk to me from your soft parts
It's enough, already, enough
         clinging to the scaffolds around the pit
Don't waste my time with the shit around the edges
Quit protecting your asshole, asshole

I've got news for you
What you think is a little sore spot
         isn't about to just heal up and leave you alone
You're sitting on a volcano
If you keep farting around like this
         you're gonna get burnt to a cinder
Then all that's left of you will be an ash
         walking around in the shape of a man

That's your choice—just don't waste my time

The fact that I'm projecting all this
doesn't let you off the hook

Quiet Zone

The kitchen is full of
yelling illegals again tonight

but behind my padded billfold
all I hear is the noisy
air conditioning, the nearly
silent passing of my own gas,
the clink of silver, laughter

What an empty protected space I have made

The Villager

Inside my fine wool suit
I am adorned with paint,
bright feathers, bits of shell

I stalk the corridors
and prowl
the cubicles

I am a gifted mimic—
my pallor is perfectly tuned
to the fluorescent lights,
I wield jargon as though
born to the blade

I have convinced even myself
that this is my place—
though at moments,
a certain
disorientation
stumbles me

and I am puzzled
to find myself barefoot
inside my shoes

The Opposite of a Vampire

What is the opposite of a vampire?
Someone you see *only* in the mirror,
who fills you with life.

That's how it was when I gave birth to my older brother.
He emerged from my side—in the mirror, not in the room.

Then he was standing beside me,
A little taller and stronger,
Wearing a beard and a baseball cap.

We were both smiling.

How It Is for the River

We learn—there must always be a space.

Sometimes it may seem that a new thing
is pushing its way in, shoving out the old.
Chances are, that's only the old in a new cloak.

Rarely a new thing will flap against the screen door,
flutter insistent wings against the window pane,
land in your hair, startle you with the
prick of its tiny claws... and fly away
when you flinch and jerk your head.

Most often, you'll never even know what flew by.

You have to make space for a new arrival.

A river only works because the water keeps moving.
All the way along the line, each moment
gives way to, draws the next: the part
at the bottom moves into the ocean,
making a space for all the other parts to move into,
all at once, each part sliding
into the space in front,
opening up a space for the next to come.

It's like that for us, but not so simple.
For us, things come in clumps, and when
we manage to get free of one thing, we find
there was a lot of other stuff connected to it,
and that stuff is gone now, too.
This is known as the clumpiness theory
of the origin of suffering.

Better than breaking free is to make
a space poised in time,
a space that is a still moment.

Imagine everything still and in motion
at the same time.

This is transparency, when the river doesn't
push at you every day,
when you are moving at the same speed
as the river.

That's how it is
for the river.

Behind the Stone

The trail is faint.

Tall trees, my elder brothers,
shape and hold close a rosary,
bells of air strung for me to tell
by stepping through them.

Each footstep drops small rustles
that quickly disappear
like morning sounds drawn down
into thick, new snow.

The quiet here is poised, the leaves
have caught their breath.
The forest is attending.

On the hilltop stands an old house.
It is bigger on the inside
than the outside.
There is fresh paint on the shutters, but
a few crumbs of bread, long dry,
lie forgotten on the dining table.
The doors and windows have long been
painted shut.

The hammering of my fists,
the tearing of my antlers
against the walls
brings no response;
the bellowing of my mouth
is ripped away by a silent wind.

Inside, the house goes on forever.

To enter, I must learn to slide myself
across the smoothest stone,
must curve my body round
to that place behind the stone
that is not behind the stone.

There, in the pure moonlight,
in the barest hint of sweet jasmine,

the perfect master

      will give me

            nothing

Coming Over the Hill

Coming over the hill this morning
you saw the mountains flung across the sky
breastbones wide
creating space for the heart to expand
the lungs to fill with icy sunlit air

The mountains breathe
at the pace of the day
inhale with the sunrise
exhale with the deepening dark

When the breaths of your life
bring you again to shaded city canyons
where towers rise up only for the bearing down
and cold air reaches in
to suck the hope
from your
warm bones

Hold on young man
the time for letting go
is not yet

Breathe with the mountains

In an open field
the mauve seedheads dance above
the thick, dreaming green

It isn't just me
The morning sky is hazy
and the air is damp

Bowl of Love

Here I am, sustained
in a golden bowl of love,
each atom of me upheld,
and I'm flailing around
like a little man in a teacup

Enough gold! Enough floating!
I want the snapping turtle
at the bottom
to take me by the ankle
and drag me under

This is what you ate.
And this, here, is what you drank.
Place credit card *here*.

This is my life now.
This red book, this crusty bread.
One now. No waiting.

How Far Can it Be to Fremont Street?

The place where my teacher sits
is just across town
up at the end of Fremont street
behind the substation

but getting there, I'll tell you,
has been like pushing against a strong wind

To get from here to there,
all I have to do is follow the map—
cross the bridge, ride the freeway,
turn here, turn here

the streets are in their places, and
the map is in the glove compartment

but the going
is in my mind

and my mind is
erased in patches

like a city of tents
in a sandstorm

Bone Woman

Bone woman
Speak from the night that holds
      the separated stones
Join with your power
      the desiccated bones

From the nightword's dark
      make flesh
And from the dawn come again,
      the dew, leaping
      into light

Bone woman
Speak from the night that holds
      my separated stones
Sing into life
      my desiccated bones

From the nightwind's breath
      make flesh
And from the dawn come again,
      the dew, leaping
      into light

Pilgrims

The one who says there is no life in rocks
     misses a lot

For example, it was a rock from the riverbed
who brought to my attention
the subtle-bodied entourage of allies
assembled for my journey's sake

These are the members of my party

One long, sinuous fish
     at home in deep water
One reindeer demon
     for the laying of contradictions
One goat demon
     for the blowing away of smoke
One hanging sloth
     drawing from each step its full measure
One single-minded crocodile
     still
One frog leaping and one fish flying, flickering
     the same
One old, dusty donkey
     to carry someone else's burdens across a dry place

Back to the river, you rock
where cool water will flow again
across your shoulders

We, too, are for the road

Aaron—In Memoriam

Aaron L. Gurner
Died on the corner
Nobody's lover
Lived with his mother
Born into trouble
Finally recovered
Love you, my brother
Never another
Aaron L. Gurner

Here

Long ago in the Illinois summer,
lying on my back, I held to
the round Earth,
arms wide in the green grass—
almost spinning off
into the endless blue,
held up and held close
by the cool warm along my body

Long after, I sat
on a Scottish hillside
the scent of heather
rough and sweet in my face
The wind drew waves
in the golden oats—
shining fur,
a great Earth pelt
magically brushed
against the grain

Tonight I stand in the Whidbey dark
lifted in every
molecule of my being
by a chorus of frogs.
Above, tracks of meteors
lance through the black like javelins
or good, straight stitches.

I've heard it said that some souls
resist incarnation. Some
bend their many lives to getting
off the wheel of rebirth.

Not me. I'm running right
back in line again for another turn.

Again! Oh, again!

Where Do You Come From?

I was sent from the planet Gazebo
to entertain at garden parties

with a flute to lure little old ladies in tennis shoes
and a lasso to ensure they don't leave
before I've read them all my latest poems

They giggle!

We end with a grand aerial procession
amateurs of the flute, tangled in rope
coiling, unfurling, lofting away into the night

If you don't know the
rocks are in your mind, you may
think they're in my head

Bobbing for Grapes

Awaking,
I find myself
on a tightrope
above a cheering crowd,
wine enthusiasts
warm together
one moment in bright sunshine

Suspended,
a last, dark bunch of grapes
hangs above me

Reaching,
arms and fingers wide, chin stretching, lifting,
throat bared, cheeks flung back like wings

Attaining,
sweet juices bursting, oh
sticky and cool, oh
laughter, oh
glorious

and into oh glorious
I vanish

Treasure

You're a doll, a real doll

You came
assaulting my defenses
and gave no quarter

We never thought we'd find each other
Now we have shifting paradigms

We'll celebrate the beginning
of the gift of each other
each year in this season
Saint Nick'll be so pleased

Your scent is in my sheets

These ravens are so
hilarious, the way they
squawk at each other,

tease one another
like kids in the back seat. Don't
make me fly up there!

Is that what you want?
Do I have to pull over
and stop the forest?

Ravens arguing
Each raucous note made of praise
Alhamdulillah!

Every Day

New life
Every day
Spring time
Gonna play

Dig deep
Water well
Fresh dirt
Clean smell

Tiny seeds
Come sprout
Stick your little
Faces out

Baby leaves
Grow green
Small buds
Make the scene

Fertilize
Pollinate
Sun shine
Sit 'n' wait

Rain fall
Come what may
Celebrate this
Birth day

Slow Fire

Fire does not stop to ask permission

Fire and the trees draw from
what is below
and release to what is above

Fire is drawn to the tree as
to a brother

A tree is a slow flame

And you
<rabbinical cadence>
are a fast tree

Breeze stirs canopy
A few leaves choose this moment
to fall together

Canopy rustles
Leaves fall, all in their silence
Forest floor rustles

How quiet these woods
Be still—you can see and hear
a single leaf drop

Cape of Blessings

Sometimes I'm just sitting in my office
working along, la-la-la la-la,
when a message from you swooshes into my inbox

Suddenly a wide place opens
in my chest

I feel dizzy, weak

I close my eyes but they leak anyway

The muscles of my mouth go tight to
hold back a vibration
that would leave me collapsed
and helpless

It doesn't work

I am helpless anyway
in the cup of your love

Enfolded
in your cape of abundant blessings

Sometimes I'm just walking down the street
minding my own business,
de de-de oh, dum de-dum de-dum

when, without warning
(sunlight on concrete, trees)
everything is one piece

Not pieces connected—
one thing, never separated

I could die happily
in a moment like this
But please—not soon!

For My Daughters

I.

howl with laughter
howl for joy

find the wild one in you

follow your bliss
follow your prey
play in the meadows
and in the streets
the libraries, studios

when you have pain—howl in pain
open your throat and your heart
make room for the power of life
to live in you

howl at the moon
understand this rich world
with all your heart
and with all your mind
and for the rest—
howl at the moon

root yourself in the earth
and let the passion of your whole being
expand you to the size of stars
in the shape of your wisdom

II.

Does your path appear to you
slow and rocky, fast or smooth?
Relativity and life demand, regardless,
that to me you will seem to be
disappearing at nearly the speed of light.

I watch as you swing up a banked curve
then down onto a straightaway,
and rocket out of sight.

The wind and sun thrill in your face,
and the cold rain.
The road is endless.
No two steps fall alike.

May your hands grasp
with the tenacity of juniper roots.
May your hands release with the grace
of the evening sky giving up the day.

I will be waiting for you
each time your orbit brings
you sweeping back around
from worlds bathed in light, or
from the dark side of the moon,
until my own life is released
into the evening sky.

No world rolls under
our six stepping feet. No man,
no dog, no planet

A natcher'l dog,
he always takes time to stop
and smell the roadkill

Husband of Gaia

Walnut-sized stones in simple settings
deep green, pale blue, dusky silver
circled close about the throat

Men haven't worn jewelry like this
since the days of Atlantis

Forest green, sky blue, electric silver,
marking a covenant of earth service

Why not Husbands of Gaia,
As we have Brides of Christ?

I think of Tom Bombadil—
though in that great, unpeopled forest
he had no need
of jewelry

Wet grass, a lichened
branch, a plastic tub, the road.
Two rusty pipes, air.

We would have called it
an empty lot. But we had
emptiness all wrong.

Map of My Heart's Desire

Turning, a quarter million miles away
one lunar crater, perfectly round
its edges perfectly sharp
and small

How elegant,
how clear

See the Man in the Earth
caught out of focus, in one
astonished moment of surprise
see his round eyes, round mouth,
out of which
vines will grow

Here a cut, a bruise
Here a terrier standing
        in the road
Here a centipede advances,
        planting many feet
Here a terrier leaping

See a man play, and
        remembering to sit,
        pass through the Buddha

See the deathwatch beetle make his meal
See the sultan on his broomstick. Fly, king!

Here a man and woman embrace—
bigger than Buddha,
        and differently bent of knee

Watch now as the volcano blows

After the clouds of rock are gone
the quiet mountains remain, softly breathing
and when the mountains are gone,
an empty space

Luminous veils drift in
like sea foam without a sea

Galaxies form

In white sprinkling, new stars come down

After Long Wandering

How many silver greys this day
at the salt shore

eight at least to glorify the clouds
four on the water
and for the coots, three
and for my head, three
and with all the others, one

When the air warms,
rich smells rise out of moist earth
and I am home, safe again
after long wandering, found again
in a place I had forgotten

Now I will rest my boots for a time
and sit while the grasses come up
green and yellow around me
I will remember the young one who set out
and feed us both
on the apples I have gathered

Some trees leaf early,
others flower first. But they
all have sap, n'est-ce pas?

Pilgrimage to Your Body

I am a pilgrim to the temple of your body.

Seven times around your circumference I walk.

I climb your hundred steps on hands and knees,
I kiss each hollowed stone and touch it with my forehead.

In the sanctuary I make offerings of coconut milk,
       silver foil and papaya.

I set incense on fire.

The shadows of the holy flame caress
       the domes and arches
            of your sacred architecture.

Choirs of monks lift a shout to wake the dead.

Woodpecker saying
his own name today in a
tree across the road

Rabbit, crocus, cloud
Brief and briefer lives, never
leave eternity

Self-Recollection

you are seeking yourself
among the trees

you seek a state

the state sought
a quantum state
oscillates
scintillates
titillates
plays peekaboo
in the bright forest

magenta, umber, turquoise
flecks and trapezoids
beak shapes and leaf shapes
trunks and branches multiply
in mirrors of your
cunning and mistaken
devising

while you seek
it hides
while you abandon seeking
it turns its back

when you are still
it is revealed

Custard pie!

Immaculate Fool

Coyote is a chicken-thief
Coyote shits in my well
To break my mind is Coyote's delight

Does Coyote have a Buddha-nature?

Owoooooooooo!

Dialing down the spectrum of the world
I sit, until I am a stained-glass window

with no stain

and no glass

I am Coyote's immaculate Fool

Precipice of the Sun

It's no good, walking away
into the sunset

There is no away

Dried flesh and picking crows
your final scene along that road

Your posture of sophistication
is just an obstacle if you love the truth

Leave that childish game now
Come walking the steep road home

Carry the smoldering coal of your heart
to the precipice of the sun, and leap!

I promise
you will kindle in that moment

this

only

moment

A Celebration of Circles

(with Tina Lear, for two voices)

Today again the Earth completes a circle
whose ends do not touch

> *But I touch the ends to my beginnings*
> *and begin another circle*

In the turnings of my spiral life
I am a wheel in a wheel in a wheel

> *Through darkness and through light I spin*
> *and weave an endless song of praise*

Alive on the breath of my breath,
the breath of my moons,
the breath of my seasons,

> *In the center of the lung of God I breathe,*
> *and I am exhaled into my birth,*
> *and inhaled into my death*

> *Today again the Earth completes a circle*
> *whose ends do not touch*

But I touch the ends to my beginnings
and begin another circle

Already Home

When the afternoon wind pushes, pushes
at tree limbs in the afternoon sun,
the moving air gives speech to pine needles,
cottonwood leaves.

They know our name. They remind us
that we cannot stay.

The train and the river,
they both go by, and they call to us—
one moaning, one repeating—
Here. Here.

Why do we say that the sound of the train
is a lonesome sound? Why does it tug
at our hearts? Because the clank of the wheels
on the joints of the rails is like
the clicking in our own joints.

Because the engine breathes and beats.

We don't know where this great being
comes from, or what it carries, or why.
The train is disappearing into the distance
and so are we.

But the river—
the river is always with us.
Always leaving, always here.
The river tugs at our ankle
and reminds us

that we are already home.